Beauty in Darkness

Finding HOPE in Distressing Times.

by

David P. Therrien

ISBN – 13: 978-1456341541
ISBN - 10: 1456341545

§

Dedication Page

This book is dedicated to my wife Donna, and my three
boys, Michael, David Jr. and Alex.
It is also dedicated to the New Hope congregation and of
course, my Lord, Jesus Christ who always shows me
beauty in my darkness.

§

Beauty in Darkness

Beauty in Darkness

May also be used in a small group setting.
There are questions for discussion on each chapter
at the end of the book.

§

Beauty in Darkness

TABLE OF CONTENTS

Introduction

It is not uncommon in our human realm of thinking to view the darkness as something bad, threatening or intimidating. We have been indoctrinated since childhood to be "afraid of the dark." It is no wonder that when we reach adulthood, the times in our lives which we consider to be dark times, we find ourselves fearful and uncomfortable.

This book, "Beauty In Darkness" is intended to shed a new light on the darkness that you may find in your own personal life. May your reading open up a new window and let in the light of God as He shows you how you can find beauty in your darkness.

§

Beauty in Darkness

CHAPTER ONE
Why the Darkness?

"When in the hopeless place, the continued hopeless place, is the very time when He will stretch forth His hand against the wrath of our enemies and perfect the work which concerneth us"

Aphra White

Tell me if these sound familiar to you. Trials of life, difficult circumstances and issues that are hard to understand. Do any of these resonate with you?

This book is intended to take those experiences and help you to see them in a different way. Living life involves perspective, and perspective is how we view things. The opposing forces that we find coming into our lives are what I am going to call "Darkness." In this first chapter we will seek to understand, "Why the Darkness?"

What is darkness? Our natural understanding of darkness would be a lack of light which results in a lack of heat, which is accompanied by coldness. Due to the nature of darkness, it can also cause a hindered mobility. It slows one down. Darkness requires a need for an artificial light source. But I think God would have a different view toward darkness.

So the Scripture is true: (John 1:5) *The Light shines in the darkness and the darkness did not overtake it.* That's the good news. Darkness is there but the light always overcomes the darkness. The question remains, "Why the darkness?" Or, "Why are there times of darkness in my life?" As we begin to answer this question, open your hearts and try to begin to change your perspective so your misery can become joy.

Now, let's rewind two thousand years and watch Jesus addressing His disciples. He is giving them a pep talk, preparing to send them out to preach the Gospel of the Kingdom. He tells them to do good by healing and preaching the Kingdom message of salvation. He reminds them they don't need to take any money, God will provide for them. If they go into a city and they are not received, just move on from there. He warns them that they are going out like sheep among wolves. He tells them it won't be easy and they'll even be hated for going in the name of Jesus, but do not fear anyone. He then gives them a special encouragement. *"What I am telling you in the dark you must repeat in broad daylight, and what you have heard in private you must announce from the housetops."* (Matthew 10:27)

For God to speak to us in the dark, He must first put us in the dark.

Why this admonition? For God to speak to us in the dark, He must first put us in the dark. He must meet us in the dark. There is something going on here that goes against the natural mindset. This is a fact we rarely consider. He may tell us things in the dark where bereavement has closed the blinds of a home and has shut out the light of the sun. Maybe the dark is where sickness has hedged you in and kept you from the stir of life. Or perhaps, a heavy sorrow or disappointment has come in like a robber and stolen away your joy for a while. The dark is the place that, naturally, we do not want to be. Yet, it is in that place that He tells us His wonderful, eternal, and infinite secrets.

Have you noticed that darkness is also an opportunity for the light to shine, as the stars of heaven? What is it that makes the stars of heaven so beautiful? It is the darkness that encompasses them.

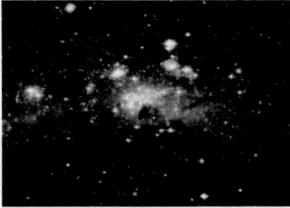

You know that the stars are there all day long, and yet, we never see them because it takes the darkness to bring out the beauty of the stars. The darkness reveals to us that the stars are there. Every clear night they call out "Look up, look at us. Aren't we beautiful? Does not the surrounding darkness bring out our beauty?"

Another aspect of the dark is that the ear gains a heightened sensitivity. In life there is commotion and the hubbub of the day. Sometimes we suffer from what is called information overload. Perhaps your life has felt like this with too many magazines, and newspapers, too many reports to read, shows to watch, and things to study. When you are in that position, how can you hear from God?

Have you experienced calendar overload? Do you have an intimate relationship with Post It notes? It is like you are being pursued by a fanatical lover. Everywhere you turn, a Post It note is there watching you. They are on the refrigerator, and the calendar. They are on your wall at work. Everywhere you turn, a Post It note is looking at you, beckoning you to give it attention. Our calendars can become so full; we don't have time for the important things, like family, fun and hearing from God. If your calendar is so full that you can't hear from God, that calendar has become your master. Rather than you master it, it now masters you. That is destructive and makes us deaf to the things that God wants to tell us.

Have you ever experienced people overload? We have too many places to go, too many things to do, and now, too many people to see. People are pulling at you from every direction. All these people in your life pulling at you, pulling at you. That's why we go on v-a-c-a-t-i-o-n! Some of you are crazy enough to bring people with you!

Is it possible you are overloaded with stuff? You have too much stuff! You really discover you have too much stuff when you get ready to move. When you are preparing to move, you find stuff you've had for five years that you didn't know you had. Then you move, take it with you, and store it away for five more years. One day you decide to throw it away and after you do, you're looking for it because you need it. I think you get the idea.

So then, why the darkness? Perhaps because we get to a place in our lives where there is too much noise, too much clutter, too much work and too much stuff, even too many people. Are you able to identify right now as you read? God has something to say. He has something special He wants you to know. He has a personal revelation for you. But if our lives are consumed with too many people, stuff, noise and busyness, how can He ever speak to us? So what does God do? He allows us to go into a place of darkness. That darkness can be a place of bereavement, sickness, trial or a storm. This does not mean you have done something wrong and you are being punished. It means that God wants your attention because He has something personal He wants to tell you.

> **"What I am telling you in the dark you must repeat in broad daylight, and what you have heard in private you must announce from the housetops."**
> **Matthew 10:27**

When you are in the darkness you can find Christ, the Light of the world there. That light brings illumination, warmth and mobility. Maybe that is the time when you are just sitting and thinking, "Hey, where is everybody? Why is there no one here to listen to me? Why is there no one here to help me? Why is there no one here to understand me? Why am I all alone in this?" Maybe, just maybe, it's the Lord Jesus that wants to come in, and He desires your total, undivided attention. You see, this goes against our natural way of thinking. We think that when things go wrong, or don't go our way, or begin to fall apart, that's bad. In reality, this is the time when Jesus Christ wants to move in and get really personal. He has something to tell you that is eternal and infinitely wise, that you need for your life.

The Bible tells us: *"The God who said, Out of darkness the light shall shine! is the same God who made his light shine in our hearts, to bring us the knowledge of God's glory shining in the face of Christ.* (II Corinthians 4:6)

If you are a believer in Jesus Christ, you have the light of God inside of you. If you are not a believer as of yet, turn to the end of this book and read what it means to become a child of God. Perhaps you are a child of God but you lack assurance regarding your relationship with Him. See "The Invitation."

When you find yourself in that dark situation, you can count on God finding you there, and He will bring His light. God has something to tell you and when He does tell you, if you listen in humility, He will light up your path. He will bring light to that darkness. That is what the Lord desires to do. He doesn't keep us in the darkness, but He meets us in the darkness. He speaks to us in the darkness. What He says to us we are to take out into the daylight and tell others testifying how good God is and what God has done for you.

Usually, when we are in the darkness, we criticize it. "O man, this stinks!" "My husband is such a jerk!" "My wife doesn't understand me." "I quit." "I'm getting another job, my boss is a monster." "The kids are driving me nuts." "This is wrong!" "The grass is burning, the flowers are dying!" "The lawn mower won't start!" "The car is leaking in the driveway." We criticize and analyze. We try to figure out what is going on. We do whatever we can naturally to rationalize it. Oh, I know why this happened, it's their fault! It's her fault. It's his fault. Perhaps, God is trying to slow you down. He wants you to know, "I'm trying to heighten your hearing. I'm shutting you out of the hubbub. I'm taking you out of the chaos. I'm shutting out the busyness of life. I've got something to say to you. It took Me putting you in this dark situation for you to hear what I've got to say to you." That's why criticizing it, analyzing it, and

6

rationalizing it away does not fulfill the purpose of God. The purpose of God is to quiet you down, to bring you to a place of complete humility where you are in such darkness that you are literally immobilized. Did you ever feel like that? I am immobilized!

Remember the story of the Exodus. One of the plagues God brought was a darkness that was so deep, not one of the Egyptians could or would go out of their houses. They were completely immobilized!

God may put you in a darkness to immobilize you so He may speak to you. He is not hurting you or punishing you. He just wants to speak to you. And do you know why? Because you need to change your perspective about something. You're looking at something the same way, all the time and it is not working. If you have an attitude toward something or someone, and it does not improve the situation, it is time to change the attitude. It is time to change your perspective. This is so important, especially in marriage. Unfortunately, Christian marriages have the same rate of failure as non-Christian marriages. There is something vitally wrong. Do you know what we need to do in our marriages? When you have an attitude toward your spouse and that attitude is not making the situation any better, you need to change your perspective, change your attitude. If you don't, God will back you up into the darkness, and it will be thick and you will be immobilized. God will say, "Now will you listen? I had to shut everything out. I had to bring you to a place where I want to tell you something because I want you to start thinking differently. I've got a secret for you that you didn't know before, and what I'm going to tell you is going to be the best thing that you could ever hear. Don't question it, rationalize it, criticize it or analyze it."

God wants to give you a revelation but the many voices of life have drowned out His voice. The many voices are your friends, that love you, but they are opinionated and not objective to truth. They can drown out the voice of God. Did you know that best friends can give the worst advice? As a matter of fact, you may not want to go to a best friend for advice because they love you and they don't want to hurt you or risk the friendship, so they will tell you something that is not right but sentimental. Perhaps even something that will hurt the situation rather than help it. They would rather be your friend, than give you the truth. If you want truth, go to someone who is not afraid to risk the friendship, who understands *"faithful are the wounds of a friend."* (Proverbs 27:6) Even well-meaning voices can drown out the voice of God.

Sometimes we don't get private with God until He puts us there.

Jesus said, *"What you have heard in private..."* (Matthew 10:27) If you are the kind of person who likes to be busy, you can become so busy that God has to put the brakes on. Nothing is working and you're wondering, questioning, analyzing, and rationalizing what's going on. Then a verse like this shows up: *"What I am telling you in the dark you must repeat in broad daylight..."* (Matthew 10:27) For God to tell me something in the darkness, He must meet me in the darkness, but first, He has to put me in the darkness.

So when I'm in the darkness, that's a good thing, because that is where God is going to meet me. Before that, I had too much stuff, noise, hubbub, and too much going on that God couldn't get my attention. He couldn't privately speak to me the deep secrets of heaven.

Sometimes in our worse situations, God has given us a revelation. He has given us a way out and now we have a testimony, something to say to someone else. We can share with other people what He has done for us. This is what brings glory to God.

Therefore, the things in our lives that we consider to be dark, meet God there. Stop pointing the finger and rationalizing. Stop putting on your cloak of self-righteousness, and humble yourself. Let God speak to you. He is going to tell you something that you never thought of, that you probably won't like. He may even give you something to do that you won't want to do, at least in your flesh. God is saying, Do you want it to stay like it is or do you want it to get better? You need to sit, listen and let Me change your perspective. Then you go at that thing and watch the difference. When God comes through, you can then glorify Him by announcing it from the housetops. Now you have a witness and a testimony to tell people what God has done for you.

God shows up in the strangest places

God met Moses in the wilderness, Gideon in a cave, Elijah at Mount Horeb, and the Apostle Paul in the desert of Arabia. These are not particularly pleasant places, but that's where they heard from God. Sometimes we think, "Oh, I'm going to go into my prayer closet because I'm spiritual and God is going to meet me in my prayer closet." Maybe He will. But God doesn't just meet you in the prayer closet. He may want you in the wilderness. He shows up in the strangest places.

When God told Elijah to meet Him in the cave on the mountain. Elijah could have said, "I'm a prophet. I don't want to go to a cave. Can't we meet at the 99 Restaurant? Oh, I know a nice place by the water. I love to eat by the water." God met Moses when he was in the wilderness, up in a mountain while shepherding sheep. God sent Paul, the great apostle, into the desert of Arabia. Do you know how hot a desert can be? God said that He would meet him there. Paul stayed there for three years and he met with God. You see, there is no shortcut to the life of faith which is the condition of the victorious life.

So the question today is, Do I want the victory over the thing that plagues me? I would think that we all want the victory because we all have a battle that we are fighting. A life of faith comes from listening to God. Sometimes God will put me in the darkness to get my attention so He can speak to me. One person said, "Some hearts, like certain flowers, open more beautifully in the shadows of life."

There is a beautiful flower called the Night Blossom. But it only opens in the dark. All during the day the flower remains closed, its beauty hidden. During the night, when all the light is gone, that beautiful flower begins to open. It takes the darkness to bring that flower to life.

There are things in your life that God wants to blossom. He wants to bring them to life, but sometimes it takes the darkness. It is not just sun all the time, nor is it rain all the time. It is a balance of everything. The times in our lives that are the darkest times are the times that God wants to say the sweetest things to us, things that will help us and change us. They will give us another way of looking at that thing, a new perspective. In humility, if you listen to God, and obey God, your life will become like that beautiful Night Blossom.

The light robs the beauty of that flower during the day, but the night time causes it to blossom and brings out its beauty. There is beauty in you because God put it there. It is a beauty that can shine in the dark times of your life. The dark times are not your enemy. They do not work against you, but are part of God's plan. Let God meet you in the darkness and speak to you there, watch the life begin to come back into you.

Human life is very busy. It goes from busy to chaotic. It's noisy and full. It's deafening and blinding. It shuts us out from those special things that God wants to tell us. So, the soul needs silence in the stir of human life. We need a time when all life can stop so the soul can hear from God, because God has something to say. Only then can the sense of God's presence become the fixed possession of our soul. God is with you all the time but do you know it? Do you sense it or feel it? Do you believe it? Sometimes we don't believe that He is there because we have been deafened to Him from the stir of life. We have even allowed the darkness to make us think it has chased God away or at least hidden Him, because we have developed a wrong perspective.

The darkness has actually created an environment where we can meet God. Unfortunately, we didn't know that because we were always afraid of the dark, or we blamed somebody for the dark. We have even blamed God for the dark. "God, why this sorrow." "Why this pain?" "Why this hurt?" "Why this loneliness?" We rationalize, criticize and analyze. Now God is saying, "I'll tell you why. It is to shut out the stir of life, so I can say something important to you."

He that has a heart of humility will listen to God.

Jesus said, *"He that has ears to hear, let him hear."* (Mark 4:9) This takes a real change of perspective because in our natural thinking, when it gets dark, we turn on a light. We don't like the dark, we prefer light. The dark immobilizes and hinders. God is saying, "But that's the place where I meet you, and the place that I speak to you."

So where does it begin? Well, it ends in the light on the rooftop, (Matthew 10:27) but it begins in the darkness with God. In times that we feel the worst, that's when God shows up and gives us what we need. We then come alive like the Night Blossom, saying, "Thank you God for the dark. Look at the beauty you have brought out of it."

Only then can the sense of God's presence become the fixed position of the soul. Our soul is to be always fixed on God. Let's all say with the psalmist; *"Thou art near, O God."* (Psalm 119:15)

§

CHAPTER TWO

"Why Pain?"

"To do and suffer God's will is still the highest form of faith."

Dr. Charles Parkhurst

Darkness is not something that we are fond of, naturally speaking. But we're learning that there is beauty in darkness. As we saw in the previous chapter, some hearts are like certain flowers, they open more beautifully in the shadows of life. In this time of reading together, we're going to answer the question "Why pain?"

Have you ever had the blessing of seeing a Night Blossom flower in the night? It is truly an unexpected sight. The beauty of this flower is not seen during the day when the light of the sun is shining. It takes a very dark time to cause this flower to bloom. It is a beautiful flower. This flower teaches us that in our own lives, it is often the darkest times that can actually cause our inner beauty to reveal itself.

Why Pain?

The common question people ask is "Why is there pain in life?" Dear readers, some of you have been waiting such a long time for that answer. "Why

Pain?" Some of you know the pain of the heart, it's breaking. Some of you know the pain of your conscience, it's haunting you. You know the pain of the body, it's aching. You may even know the pain of God's plan for your life, it's mystifying. You haven't been able to figure it out yet.

Let's take a journey back through time to the land of Uz. Perhaps you have heard about this place. It is an old place that holds a popular story about a man named Job. We are going to see a life that was filled with blessing like the forest is filled with trees. He was a man who had everything his heart desired, for a time. Then, God called Job into the darkness.

Job knew suffering. As a matter of fact, that is what has made him so well known, even today. Perhaps you have even heard the expression, "The suffering of Job." Job knew the pain of heartache. He suffered the loss of all of his livestock, servants, crops, and even his children. He also suffered the pain of an aching body, for the story tells us that he was struck with sores and boils over all of his body. He suffered from a haunting conscience from so-called best friends who condemned him, pointing their fingers at him, telling him that his present situation was his own doing. He suffered the pain of God's plan. What was going on! It was a mystery, even to Job. It was a great mystery because Job was a righteous man. We sometimes think that in our good behavior we will always experience good things and good times. Oh, how our natural thinking can sometimes trick us to the true reality.

Have you ever thought to yourself or said to someone, "I'm a good person, why do I hurt?" Or thought, "What have I done to deserve this?" Yet, in his own righteousness, Job suffered all of these things. How did this darkness creep into Job's life?

Well, here is the story. Satan came before God one day and said, "I'll tell You why Job loves You. Because you have blessed him with wealth, children, livestock and servants. You have made him a very wealthy man. He does not lack one thing. Of course he loves You!" Then God said to Satan, "Have your way with him. Do what you will with him, but spare his life. We will watch his response to these sufferings in the human realm." (Job 1:1-12)

Darkness crept in. Job became a bankrupt man. Life was no longer as he knew it. Everything had changed! Yet in spite of all of this adversity, Job still trusted God.

There are things in life that are very good, according to the natural eye. But sometimes they do not look that good when we hold them up to the mirror of God's plan.

What is good in the natural, may not be necessarily good in the spiritual.
What is good in the spiritual, may not be necessarily good in the natural.

What was happening to Job in the natural would not be considered good. But to God, it was good because it had a purpose. When we find ourselves in these places of darkness, it is easy to come up with all kinds of responses. We can have various reactions to the pain that we are suffering even when we are doing the best that we can. I want you to think of what Job said about his painful reality. *"It is easy to condemn those who are suffering when you, yourself have no troubles."* (Job 12 CEV). Job is saying that people don't care about your troubles, but they don't mind condemning you for them. When we really hurt deeply, most people do not care. They have enough trouble of their own than to get involved with the trouble of someone else. How often have we heard sad stories of people in need being left on a sidewalk of a busy city and no one stops to help? So Job is saying that when you have troubles and you are hurting, expect to go through it without a lot of help.

Job continues his commentary and says, *"The tents of the destroyers prosper, and those who provoke God are secure, whom God brings into their power."* (Job 33:22) What is Job saying here? It seems as though God keeps the wicked safe. A question was asked generations later by King David, *"How long shall the wicked triumph?"* (Psalm 94:3) You have probably asked that question. You have seen some people in the world and in your life and think to yourself, "Why do they have so much?" "Why do the good people seem to die and why does God prosper these evil people?" In his suffering, Job made the same observation. That is why God's plan is very mystifying.

But Job seems to be working out the answer. God comments, *"Ask the beasts, and let them teach you; and the birds of the heavens, and let them tell you. Or speak to the earth, and let it teach you; and let the fish of the sea declare to you. Who among all these does not know that the hand of the LORD has done this?"* (Job 12:7) What is God telling Job, but that the whole world knows that God is working? The whole creation knows that God has a plan and that God is doing something. EVERYBODY KNOWS THIS JOB, EXCEPT YOU! All creation knows that God is working and He is carrying out His plan for your life.

If you are familiar with the story, you know that after his great loss, Job is sitting in a dump, a landfill, covered with sores and boils. He is probably sitting on a rock and look, he is scraping dry skin off of his body with a piece of broken pottery, (Job 2:8) and contemplating the fact that everything is gone. At one point, he was at the highest place you could be in life and now he is at the lowest place, perhaps even a breath away from giving up, even near death. That is what his life has been reduced to. To think, the hand of the Lord has done this! (Job 12:9) What does God want Job to know, but that He is making Job into greatness!

Now, is there any way you can see similar circumstances in your own life? Is it possible for you to see that your adversity is God's plan to turn you into someone great? I wonder sometimes if spiritual truth is based on natural truth or is natural truth based on spiritual truth. They seem to coincide with one another.

Let's look at the diamond.

Notice the diamond, freshly cut from the ground. It is beautiful, but it hasn't yet reached its potential. This rough cut diamond is very similar to you and me. We are beautiful because we are created in the image of God, but we are marred because of sin. We are not shining in all of our brightness and all of our glory like we should be. The good news is that God loves us so much, that He doesn't leave us that way. So, as with any rough cut diamond, the lapidary goes to work. He is not satisfied with the shape of the diamond. He goes into his tool box and prepares his tools so he can turn this rough cut diamond into an object of beauty and something that is even more valuable than it is in its present state. He opens his toolbox, retrieves his tools and begins to work.

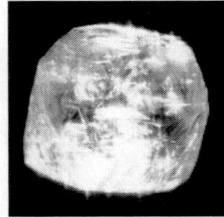

One of the tools that he has, believe it or not, is a saw blade. The first word that may come to your mind when you discover that a saw blade is one of his tools is "ouch." Why a saw blade? The saw blade is that which he uses to cut a notch into the diamond. A saw blade is very intimidating. It would cause one to fear, to wonder. He then goes back into his toolbox and retrieves his sculpting tools. When a diamond cutter takes that rough stone and turns it into something beautiful, he needs a hammer and chisels of all sizes and types. He knows exactly what he is going to do. He is going to chip away that which is in that diamond that doesn't belong there. Every diamond that is found in the ground has flaws that don't belong there and hinder its beauty.

Every human being has something in them that doesn't belong there. It's called a flaw. God must go into His toolbox and select the proper tools to remove that flaw. He takes out the saw, hammer and chisels and goes to work. He begins the process of removing the things that obscure your beauty.

If we looked at the whole set of tools in the tool box with the eyes of a rough cut diamond, and saw those weapons of mass destruction, we would say, "I wish I were something else." When you understand that God has a toolbox to work in your life, you think to yourself, "That's for me?"

Don't you love it when you go to the dentist and all the tools are lined up on that little porcelain shelf next to your chair? You think to yourself, "That's for mc?" There are all shapes and sizes of picks and sharp, pointy things that are going to be jabbed into your mouth. It is all to work on you, for your good! Likewise, the toolbox for the rough cut diamond represents the plan of God for your life. Just like every tool is different in size and use, the

18

lapidary uses them all to shape that diamond. So is it with us. God has various ways of working in all of our lives. His assorted tools in His toolbox are simply the plan of God for each one of us.

You may hear this and think to yourself, I don't think I like that. The good news is that God knows what He is doing.

A lesson on diamond cutting.

The way a diamond is cut impacts its brilliance. A poorly cut diamond is less luminous. Therefore, the more skill and the better the tools, the better the cut and the more brightly shining will be the diamond. If the lapidary, however, is not that skilled and his tools are not that sharp, it will reflect light less and the diamond will lose its beauty and value. The beauty in the diamond is in its ability to reflect light. The clearer the diamond the more it will be able to reflect light and bring a greater price. It is not so much the size of the diamond but the clarity of the diamond. It is the purity of the diamond that gives it its beauty.

The cut is then determined, not by what the lapidary wants it to be, but rather by the shape and location of the internal flaws. The diamond cutter doesn't take the diamond and say, "I want this diamond to be such and such," and then shapes it into whatever he wants it to be. Instead, he studies the diamond intently and then goes about his work to remove all the flaws and imperfections. Whatever the gem turns out to be, that's what it is going to be. So his number one responsibility is not to shape it the way he wants to but to remove everything that is wrong with it. And by removing everything that is wrong with it, it begins to take on its own shape, perhaps even a shape that is more surprising than originally thought. Therefore, it is the flaws in the diamond that determine the cut.

Now he goes to work. The lapidary puts a notch in the diamond, just a little, tiny notch, using his sharp saw blade. He then strikes that notch with a hard blow using the hammer and chisel. The stone now lies in two.

The uninformed mind says, "Oh no, what are you doing! You had this big beautiful diamond, now you have two little ones. What a waste!" The uninformed mind thinks, the bigger the diamond, the more value it has. You see, the uninformed mind is usually wrong, because it is uninformed. The natural mind is usually wrong when it comes to the things of God. Actually, the natural mind is always wrong when it comes to the things of God because God's mind is spiritually discerned. So the natural mind says, "Oh, he just ruined the diamond! He took one big one and made two little ones."

Can you see the lapidary smiling? He is the one with the informed mind. You see, before he put that notch in the diamond, and hit it with his hammer and chisel; he did something that the uniformed mind had not considered. He studied the diamond intently. From what he saw in the diamond, he planned what he was going to do with it. He made drawings of it. He made models of it. He looked at it from every angle. He studied it deeply and intently. He knew everything about that rough cut diamond before he went to work. Then, after studying it completely, the plan was developed and he knew exactly where to strike the stone to bring the best result.

The rough cut diamond was in the hands of a man with great wisdom, skill and the best tools. The blow to the diamond was not a mistake, but rather, it was a demonstration of the diamond cutter's skill.

Let's rewind.

Remember Job sitting in the landfill? He lost all he once had and was sick with sores and boils over his body. Someone would look at Job and say, "What a mistake. What a waste." "This should not have happened." But that is what the uninformed mind says. The life of Job was not a mistake, nor were the circumstances of his life. Job's life is submitted to the toolbox of God. And as the professional lapidary who knew the rough cut diamond inside and out, God knew Job inside and out. God studied Job and knew exactly what to do with him in order to bring him to greatness. And as the Divine Lapidary, God knew where to strike him to bring him to greatness. That was God's plan for Job.

When the lapidary struck that little stone, he did what needed to be done to bring it to its perfect shape, greatest radiance and splendor. But what does it take to go from the rough cut diamond to the beautiful gem? It takes a skilled lapidary, who studies, plans, saws, notches, hammers. and chisels all the way through until the process is finished.

So what does this have to do with us?

The answer is found in Psalm 103:14 which says, *"He knows our frame and He is mindful that we are but dust."* Jeremiah 29:11 tells us, *"For I know the plans that I have for you, declares the LORD, plans for welfare and not for calamity to give you a future and a hope."* God knows how we are made, what we are made of and He has a plan. His plan is to bring us to brilliance, radiance and greatness. He knows everything about us. He knows how we think, how we feel, what makes us tick. He knows what makes us happy and sad. He knows the whole thing! And He has that toolbox called "life events." Those events also consist of people and how they treat us, at the right time and just in the right place, He strikes us to begin the beautification process. Then we question it and ask, "Why pain?" The pain is the pathway to greatness.

Sometimes God lets a stinging blow fall upon your life and everything starts to shake. You are reeling; you don't know what to do. You ask, "What just hit me?" "How did this happen?" The blow seems to be a huge mistake.

You think to yourself, "I'm a good person. How could God let this happen to me?" "Why would God do this to me?" It is not a mistake. God doesn't make mistakes. God is the Perfect, Divine Lapidary and He knows what He is doing.

You are the most precious jewel in the world to God. He is the most skillful lapidary in the universe. So when you take that rough cut diamond and put it in the diamond cutter's hand, what do you think he is going to do with the diamond? Hang it up on the wall? Put it in the counter in the jewelry store? No, no, no. He is going to go to work. And he is going to cut and saw and shape and chisel and hammer and do everything that needs to be done because he wants to bring that rough cut stone to its greatest radiance and brilliance. And that takes a lot of work!

Now, enter into the hands of the Divine Lapidary. God loves you too much to leave you in your rough cut condition. He will take out His toolbox and go to work. He is going to cut, saw, shape, chisel, hammer and do everything that needs to be done because he wants to bring you, that rough cut stone, to as much radiance and brilliance as possible. It takes a lot of work! And unfortunately, it takes a lot of pain.

God said to Isaiah, the Old Testament prophet, *"It is I who made the earth and created man upon it. And I stretched out the heavens with my hands and I ordain all their hosts."* (Isaiah 45:12) What is God saying? God is saying that He is the Divine Architect, Builder and Assembler. He is the Divine Sustainer. It is all about God. The best thing that we can do for ourselves is to start thinking with God, and thank Him for finding you, though a rough cut stone. He is going to make you into a beautiful, radiant, precious gem. When God takes out His toolbox, trust Him because He knows what He is doing.

Why the pain? When the flaws are removed, the diamond shines in all of its brilliance. The difference between the finished diamond and the rough cut one is that everything that was wrong with it has been removed. The flaws and imperfections have been removed. All that which was robbing it of its beauty has been removed. Now, what is left is purity and clarity. The way that it has been cut causes it to reflect the light beautifully, which has also added tremendous value.

"For we have this treasure in earthen vessels, that the surpassing greatness would be of God and not of ourselves."
II Corinthians 4:7

There is greatness inside of you. God put that greatness there. There is something beautiful and luminous. It is a treasure. God's treasure is inside of you. The day you gave your life to Jesus is the day God put that treasure inside of you. It is beautiful, but now He wants to get it out. Like that alabaster box of perfume that the woman broke to anoint Jesus, when she did, the fragrance filled the room. (Mark 14:3) We are a lot like that alabaster box. It is when we are broken that the treasure flows out.

Why pain? Because it is when the rough cut diamond is placed in the lapidary's hand that he works that diamond. Eventually, the beauty and radiance begins to shine. It takes pain to get there. God is making you right now, in your life, into greatness. And do you know what you are doing? You are quarreling with the process. You are telling the Great, Divine Lapidary, He is making a mistake. He is doing it all wrong! "Hey, that's not right!" Sometimes we just say, "That's not fair! I don't deserve this!" We say, "I deserve better." That is how we rationalize when we don't agree with the way God is working in our lives. Remember, He is making you into greatness and this is the process.

Let the Maker handle you as the potter does the clay. When the clay submits to the potter, a beautiful vessel comes out, fit for the king. The jewel smith handles the gem. Yield yourself to the hands of the Divine Lapidary. Let God complete His work. An unfinished work is a sorry sight. Whether it is a meal, a painting or even a load of laundry, when it remains unfinished, it has no beauty. God began a work in you and the more you cooperate with God's divine plan, the sooner He will complete the work that He began. Then you will be able to say, like Job, "The hand of the Lord has done this."

Do you think that would be a better response, than, "I don't deserve this," or "That's not fair?" How about trying, "The hand of the Lord has done this." That's what Job discovered. The heart pain that you are feeling right now, that aching pain, emotional pain or social pain, could that possibly be the hand of the Lord? Can you say "The hand of the Lord has done this to bring me to greatness?"

If you recognize that it is God who is working in your life that way, you will be wise and shine like the stars of heaven. God is looking for radiant people. He is looking for brilliantly shining people, and this is the path we must take to get there.

§

CHAPTER THREE

"Seeing God In The Darkness"

"See God in everything and God will calm and color all that thou dost see."

H.W. Smith

Did you ever notice how difficult it is to see in the dark? Many things are difficult, if not impossible to see in darkness. But the good news is, that which shines brightly in the darkness can actually be seen "in a better light", such as, the stars of heaven. The darkness of the night allows for the beauty of the stars of heaven.

You are deep below the earth in a mine shaft, mining for gold. It is dark down there and beginning to get a little colder. But you are there because you are seeking treasure. It is a valuable prize you are after and you are ready to risk life and limb to attain it. As you read this book, you are risking, not life and limb, but perhaps even more.

You are risking many of your preconceived notions about life and how life should be. You are even risking your thoughts about God and how God should be. By keeping at the task, you have found a nugget. Look at what is written on the nugget.

Even during the darkest times of our lives, there is beauty.

Sometimes, in the darkest time when you cannot see anything else, you can actually see God. Well, I don't mean that you can actually see Him physically, but you know that He is near. Maybe, just maybe, God is the only one that He wants you to see. In that darkness, everything is blocked out, and all we can see is Him, like the bright shining stars of heaven.

Just like looking at the stars of heaven, we have to look up. If you're going to find God in the dark time of your life, you have to look up at Him. Now, here is the problem. In the dark times of our lives, rather than looking up at Him, we look down. You'll never see God looking down, when the place to see Him is looking up.

Sometimes, during those dark times we look around. We look at our circumstances and we become overwhelmed with what is happening in our lives and with what is going on around us. But even by looking around, you are not looking up to where God is.

Sometimes during those dark times, we look within. We look within ourselves, and we try to figure out what is going on inside. "Why do I feel the way I feel?" "Why do I think the way I think?" But even by looking within, you're not going to see God in the darkness. In order to see God in the darkness, you have to look up at God, not around, not down, and not even within.

Here comes the night.

As the day draws to a close, it seems as if the entering darkness is chasing away the sounds of the day. It becomes quiet at night. Hustle and bustle move out and silence moves in. If you live in the country, you may hear the creatures of the night, but things do seem to quiet down. The good news is, there is a song that is heard at night that is most beautiful. It is sung by one bird, the nightingale, aptly named so. The word "nightingale" means songstress. The nightingale is a bird that sings only at night. Interestingly, the song is sung by the male. Mrs. Nightingale doesn't sing that much. It is the male nightingale that has the song. Perhaps God has a lesson for us in this operatic friend. It is a lesson just for men. Men, when you are in the dark time of your life, don't whine, sing. Don't complain, sing. Maybe God is showing us through nature that in the dark times, men need to be men. We don't need to be wimping around, crying on people's shoulders. We need to sing in the darkness. And did you know that the more noise that is around, the louder the nightingale sings. The more disturbances are present, the louder he sings. He will not let the sounds of the evening drown out his song.

Imagine being the kind of person that won't let the events of your life or the chaos of the day drown out your song. Maybe the worse things get, the louder you will sing. Chaos and disturbance only heighten your song. The more things seem to be working against you, the more beautiful is your song.

Louder, louder and louder.
Sings the nightingale.

And that nightingale song is beautiful in the darkness of the night. Even more beautiful than any other sound you would hear in the dark.

So the sight shows you certain things that can only be seen in the darkness. The hearing of the ear can testify of things that can only be heard in the darkness. But, what about the smell?

The Rose.

There is a certain rose that is grown in the Balkan mountains of Bulgaria, that is used to make an extremely fragrant and expensive perfume. This rose is gathered at night between one and two o'clock in the morning. You would think that is a strange time to go out and gather roses. Why are they gathered in the middle of the darkest part of the night? Why is this work carried out during such an inconvenient time? This is the time the flower is closed, and when it is closed, it keeps in all of its fragrance. The reason this particular rose is harvested, is because it is used to make an extraordinary perfume. In the darkest time of the night, the flower is the most fragrant. So that is when it is gathered. Some scientists say that forty percent of the fragrance of roses disappears in the light of the day.

Ladies, when you are given a rose, what is the first thing you do? You probably smell it. You smell it because of the fragrance. But it is in the night time that the rose has the greatest fragrance. So, if he really loves you, he'll show up at one o'clock in the morning and bring you your rose. And if you love him, you won't slam the door in his face for waking you up. It is in the beauty of the darkness that brings out the greatest fragrance of the rose.

The Sorrowful Tree

There is a tree that is called, "The Sorrowful Tree." It is a singular shrub that grows on an island near the city of Bombay, India. At sunset, no flowers are found on this tree. The good news is, thirty minutes after the setting of the sun, blossoms begin to appear on the tree one by one, like the stars in the night sky. These blossoms yield a sweet odor to the fortunate passerby. When the light of the day begins to break forth, the blossoms either fall off or close up. Thus, every night it continues to flower. It is called the Sorrowful Tree because we equate darkness with sorrow. God is showing us, even through this friendly fern, that darkness can be a time of beauty and sweet fragrance. Nature itself shows us darkness can be a time of shining and singing. We truly need a deeper understanding of the mystery of the darkness.

What about the darkness in my life?

How do I really see the darkness in my life? Is there really beauty in my darkness? For the Christian, there is phenomenal beauty in the dark times of our lives, if we learn to look for that beauty.

It was when darkness fell upon the earth that Jesus hung on the cross to atone for our sins. (Matthew 27:45-46) That was the beauty in the darkness. It was also in that time of darkness and tremendous sorrow that God was reconciling the world back to Himself. It was in that time of darkness that the Roman Centurion realized and said, *"Truly, this man is the Son of God."* (Matthew 27:54) In that very dark time, Jesus Christ was emitting the character of His Father. He was the fragrance of God. The fragrance was so sweet that a pagan, Roman soldier would look up and say, "Fellows, this is God!"

How does this work for us?

We have seen that even the natural world reveals there is beauty in darkness. In His own darkness, Jesus Christ, Himself, revealed that God was in Him, and He was God.

You may be familiar with Daniel and the story of the lion's den. (Daniel 6:16) The good news is, God was working. Though Daniel was in a very dark place, a place of intimidation and danger, God was working on behalf of him, and spared him.

Being in the furnace of fire was a dark time for the three Hebrew boys. (Daniel 3:21) The good news is that God was working and God spared them. God spared them to the degree that when they came out of the furnace the smell of smoke could not even be detected on their clothes!

In ancient Egypt, a darkness fell upon the earth that was so thick, no one went out of their houses. The good news is, God was working and His people had light in their homes! You see, when you are in the darkness and you know God is working, you will see the beauty in the darkness. Sometimes, God works very slowly, and meticulously. Picture someone fixing a watch. Slowly and meticulously, that's how the watchmaker works, because it is a complicated piece with much detail.

Have you ever watched someone diffuse a bomb in a movie? This is not done in a careless fashion. Did you ever think that God working in you could be like diffusing a bomb? God is working, especially in your dark times. If you are having a hard time seeing God, know that God is seeing you. You don't have to doubt or be fearful. You only have to let God do His work and bring you through.

The stories of the Old Testament were recorded for our encouragement. (Romans 15:4) They are stories about overcomers. What makes a person an overcomer? It is faith in God that makes you an overcomer. The Bible tells us, *"For whatever is born of God overcomes the world; and this is the victory that has overcome the world--our faith."* (I John 5:4)

If I am to be an overcomer in this world, then I need to be born of God. That happens when I put my faith in Jesus Christ and I believe that He is God come in the flesh to die for the sins of the world, including mine. I believe in my heart, You died for me. You shed Your blood for me and I want You in my life. I'm believing on You as my Lord and Savior. At that moment I am born of God and His Spirit comes to live inside of me, and I become an overcomer! (Ephesians 4:30)

You see, we don't need more intelligence, we need faith. We don't need more money, we need faith. We don't need more muscle, influence, joy, or friends. We need faith, faith in Him who loves us, died for us, and wants us to be overcomers in this world. Faith looks to God and no one else. I'm not looking down, I'm not looking around, and I'm not looking within. I'm looking up to God. That's faith.

Faith pleases God. (Hebrews 11:6) It is in the darkness that we exercise our faith.

Let your song be at night, as well as during the day. Don't let circumstances dictate to you when you are going to sing. Don't let events tell you when to be happy or when to be sad. Don't let what happens to you control your emotions. Faith tells me, God is watching, He is with me, and He is working. Maybe I'm having a hard time seeing Him, but He can certainly see me. Faith and nature tell me beautiful things happen in the darkness. If I know God and I trust God in my darkness, He can cause some wonderful things to happen for me.

Do you doubt God is there?

God is Spirit and we cannot see Him with the human eye but nature reveals Him. *"For since the creation of the world His invisible attributes, His eternal power and divine nature, have been clearly seen, being understood through what has been made, so that they are without excuse."* (Romans 1:20) Who God is has been clearly revealed in nature, and God teaches us through nature. Therefore, there is no excuse! We are living in an environment that testifies to the existence of God, and life lessons are all around us.

"The heavens are telling of the glory of God. Their expanse is declaring the work of His hands." (Psalm 19:1) Even the huge heavens are just a small part of who God is. Think of it. The heavens are the fingerwork of God. It is only needlepoint to Him. But sadly, not many people are looking for the God who gives songs in the night. They are looking either for a God to take away the night or they are looking to see how they can get themselves out of the night. Our prayer is usually: God, take away

this darkness. Perhaps our prayer should be: God, give me a song to sing in the dark. When I can sing a song in the dark like that nightingale, that's faith, and faith pleases God.

God is looking for people that have a faith that sticks with Him. He is looking for people who do not turn their back and run. He is looking for people who really do put their lives into His hands.

"For the eyes of the LORD run to and fro throughout the whole earth, to give strong support to those whose heart is blameless toward him."
II Chronicles 16:9

Have you ever been in a prison? What about a dungeon? How about a Roman dungeon about two thousand years ago? Paul and Silas in Acts 16 were imprisoned in such a place. After being mocked, arrested, and beaten, they found themselves singing their song in the darkness at midnight. Do you know what happened? God honored their song of faith and sent an angel to set them free. Perhaps you, dear reader, need to be set free. You know deep down within your heart something is there that is holding you hostage. You are in a prison. You are in bondage to a behavior or a thought process. It might be a way of life or a particular bias toward life. Perhaps it is a spirit of criticism or selfishness. It could be anything that has robbed your freedom. It might be really dark to you, but if you can exercise faith and sing your song in the night, God will set you free.

God hasn't called you to live in bondage. He has called you to live in faith. If the nightingale knows enough to sing in the night time, are you not wiser? How did you react in your last hour of darkness? Did you complain, cry, criticize someone, light up a cigarette, or get a beer? Did you shop, open a bag of nacho chips, or seek freedom in sleep? Have you thought about operating in faith and trusting God? Can you say, "God, You're the One who gives me a song in the night. Give me a song to sing." You are asking God to make you shine like the stars of the night sky. When the night is the darkest, the stars shine the brightest. This is how we find beauty in the darkness.

Solomon called Jesus, The Rose of Sharon. Jesus blossomed as God in the night season. We know that all through the three year ministry of Jesus, He was much like His Father. He taught with words of wisdom. He showed compassion. He lived in love and grace toward others. I would say, He was never more like God than in His own night season as He hung on that Roman cross of crucifixion. Do you see Him on the cross, surrounded by accusers? Yet, He is being unjustly accused. He is being mocked by others who are walking by saying, If you are God, then take yourself down. He saved others. Can he not save himself? He is a phony, a hypocrite. He is of the devil himself. Look at the Roman soldiers at the foot of the cross, gambling for his garments! They are stealing His clothing, all that He has left. With all of this going on, Jesus could actually say from the cross, *"My Father in heaven, please forgive them."* (Luke 23:34)

I don't think one can be any more like God than when one forgives. The highlight of the life of Jesus was in the darkest time of His life. Dear reader, the highlight of your life may be in your darkest time. It is in the darkness that we shine the brightest. Do not those in the world take notice of someone who loves God when things are difficult rather than when things are easy? When things are challenging you, people take notice.

Divorce is a dark and painful time. But even in that, you can find God in the darkness. God can show you beauty in your darkness. If you can come to understand the darkness, you will not fear the darkness. In fact, with God you can find beauty in darkness because God often does His best work in the darkness.

Finally, if you want God to give you a song to sing in the night season, you first have to lay down the grudge. You have to put away the attitude. You cannot be in a place of bondage and sing a song of victory. They don't travel together. You see, triumph comes after the challenge and victory comes after the battle. You cannot have a victory without a battle. Sometimes we run from the battle and God says, "I want to give you a victory. I want to give you a song. But you're running from the very thing that will enable you to sing that song which no one else can sing but you. It is your song in the night." And that song in the night that you sing will bring glory to God.

Even an angel cannot sing your song. He would have to pass through the darkness in order to do so. Angels are creatures of light. They don't enter into darkness. They don't have the opportunity to be in the valley. Angels cannot be in the darkest of times where God can give them a song in the night. But you can. When you see God in the darkness, you are being educated for the heavenly choir. Angels may reach the heights of the scale, but there are depths which belong to you. Only you can sing the low notes, because you have been there. There are notes which can only be reached by you because of your experiences.

(Streams In The Desert)

You see, there is beauty in darkness. God can give you a testimony. God can give you a song. Angels dwell in the lofty place and sing the high notes, but you can sing from the bowels of your own soul. You can sing from deep, deep within. That is where the passion is, where the emotion is. The Father is training you for the part the angels cannot sing. Like the song of the nightingale, the song that you learn in the darkness will be a sweet melody to God whom you have now seen and trusted.

There is a reason for and a purpose to this darkness. The darkness of the night allows the beautiful stars of the night to shine in all their glory. The darkness of the night brings out the song of the nightingale which fills the air with a sweet melody. The darkness of your life allows you to sing a song from the deepest part of your soul which will bring glory to God, the number one reason why we are on this earth.

§

CHAPTER FOUR

"Deliverance In The Darkness"

"He is not looking for great men, but He is wanting men who will dare to prove the greatness of their God."

A.B. Simpson

Sometimes we put God in a box, meaning that we think we know Him but our knowledge is very limited. It is very surprising to discover that God is bigger than our knowledge of Him and multifaceted. This chapter has some surprising information about our God that you may have never considered before. Please be open-minded.

God has many vocations. You would think being God is enough to keep one busy. He is a fruit inspector, (Luke 3:9) *"Indeed the axe is already laid at the root of the trees; so every tree that does not bear good fruit is cut down and thrown into the fire."* He is a builder, (Matthew 16:18) *"I will build My church; and the gates of Hades will not overpower it."* Do you know who the church is? The church is comprised of every believer in Jesus Christ in every location. God is building us together. To build something is to take many separate parts and put them together as one.

He is an architect, (Hebrews 11:10) *"for he {Abraham} was looking for the city which has foundations, whose architect and builder is God."* The secret that Abraham possessed which allowed him to continue to go forward in life was that he wasn't looking for what man could do. He was looking for what God and God alone could do.

What are you looking for in your life? Are you looking for something that man can do? If so, you will be disappointed. Are you looking for something that you can do? You will be disappointed. The secret to going forward is to look for that which God and God alone can do.

With all of the things God does, perhaps the most beneficial to us is the fact that God is a Deliverer. As we bring this writing "Beauty In Darkness" to a close, I want you to see that you have "Deliverance in the Darkness." Sometimes we enter into a dark situation and think "This is it!" "It's over!" "It's done!" "I can't go on any farther!" We must remember that it is in the darkness that God often does His best work. When we look for God in the darkness, we will find the beauty in the darkness. There is a song in the Old Testament that can help us to understand this.

"For though the LORD is exalted, Yet He regards the lowly, But the proud He knows from afar." (Psalm 138:6) The "lowly" are the humble who can be taught. They say, "I don't have all the

answers." God pays attention to this person, but He stays far from the proud.

"Though I walk in the midst of trouble, You will revive me; You will stretch forth Your hand against the wrath of my enemies, And Your right hand will save me."

"The LORD will accomplish what concerns me; Your lovingkindness, O LORD, is everlasting; Do not forsake the works of Your hands." Psalm 138:6-8

Let's go back to verse 7.

"Though I walk in the <u>midst</u> of trouble, You will revive me; You will stretch forth Your hand against the wrath of my enemies, And Your right hand will save me."

Now, what does it mean when the Bible says "Though I walk in the midst of trouble?" Dear reader, you may have, yourself, been in the midst of trouble. You know what it is to be right in the thick of it, as the heart is in the center of your body. This is being in the middle of trouble. I look forward, backward, to the side, and see only trouble. I am in the midst of trouble. Back to the song. *"Though I walk in the midst of trouble, You will revive me;"*

The "midst of trouble" is the hopeless place. Let's note some images of the hopeless place. For the army of Israel, it was a hopeless place when the giant Goliath appeared on the scene. His rants and raves struck fear into the hearts of the Israeli soldiers. He stood nine feet six inches tall and carried a huge shield and a very long spear. His voice was loud, mean and insulting. He was a picture of extreme intimidation. To some, the hopeless place is the place of intimidation. When you are intimidated, you are made to feel less than what you really are.

For others, the hopeless place is the tomb, an unwanted ending. When Lazarus had died, Martha, his sister thought the time of deliverance had passed. (John 11) She was in the hopeless place. You see, here is the beautiful thing about God.

It is never too late.
God delivers in the midst
of darkness.

God delivers in the midst of intimidation and unwanted endings. Moses and the people that came out of Egypt found themselves in a threefold hopeless place. It was made up of the mountains on either side, the Red Sea before them, and Pharaoh's attacking army coming from behind. The mountains on either side represented the great obstacles in life. Did you ever hear that phrase, "I've got another mountain I have to climb"?

The Red Sea was an impassable barrier. It is another obstacle to overcome. This barrier represents the unknown future. What is on the other side? Did you ever think to yourself, the future doesn't look good? "I don't like the future. I don't know what it holds for me." But you see, that is the place of deliverance.

Now, here comes Pharaoh's attacking army from behind. Let's watch these Hebrews. Here they come, singing and rejoicing in the great Exodus from Egypt, ending four hundred years of slavery. They have the mountains on both sides, the Red Sea before them and the oppressive Egyptians coming up behind them. They were in a hopeless place.

Perhaps this represents a time in your life you had or may even have right now; barriers on both sides, the unknown future before you and

41

oppression coming up behind you. Well, let's take a look at this story of the Hebrews. As we read through the stories of the Bible, we find that their stories are our stories! They are lived out by other people, but the incidents we read about are so similar to our own life situations. How many times could we put our name in some of the circumstances? You may read and say, "Hey, that's me. That's how I feel. It looks like I'm going through that very same thing." And we can really develop an intimacy with the people of these Old Testament times. Notice how the story unfolds here.

"As Pharaoh drew near, the sons of Israel looked, and behold, the Egyptians were marching after them, and they became very frightened;" (Exodus 14:10) They were afraid. Something bigger, badder and stronger was right on their heels, and they were afraid. *"So the sons of Israel cried out to the LORD."*

"Then they said to Moses," Now, watch what fear gets people to do. Fear gets you thinking – without God! You have laid aside who God is, and what God can do. They said to Moses,

"Is it because there were no graves in Egypt that you have taken us away to die in the wilderness? Why have you dealt with us in this way, bringing us out of Egypt?" (Exodus 14:11) They didn't understand that God was bringing them out of Egypt to give them freedom. Life is about freedom. For those of you that have received Jesus Christ as Savior, you have found freedom. And yet, some people think if I become a Christian I've got to become religious and that means no freedom. What they don't understand is that they need to become a Christian so they *can* be free. You become free from the wrath that sin deserves and free from the

power of sin that has you in bondage right now. The people gave Moses an, "I told you so" speech.

"Is this not the word that we spoke to you in Egypt, saying, 'Leave us alone that we may serve the Egyptians'? For it would have been better for us to serve the Egyptians than to die in the wilderness."

Exodus 14:10-12

They told Moses they would rather be slaves than die. We would rather be slaves than be brought into a place where we can do nothing but trust God.

Dear reader, are you like that? Would you rather be a slave to a lifestyle that is confining or controlling? Do you want an existence that only knows limitations? Does having the freedom to trust, risk, and journey into the unknown strike fear in you in any way? Do you live a life where there is no faith in God required? Could the theme song for your life be, "Rock the boat, don't rock the boat baby?" Don't make any waves in my life. Leave me alone. I'm okay in my little lifestyle. Don't put me in a place where I have to live in faith and trust God. That was the thinking of the Hebrews. Don't take us out of our comfort zone. They had forgotten that they had no comfort in that existence. They were under harsh taskmasters.

"For it would have been better for us to serve the Egyptians than to die in the wilderness." (Exodus 14:11) They had also not yet learned that the darkest time is God's time for deliverance.

The Deliverance

"But Moses said to the people, "Do not fear! Stand by and see the salvation of the LORD which He will accomplish for you today; for the Egyptians whom you have seen today, you will never see them

43

again forever. "The LORD will fight for you while you keep silent." (Exodus 14:13-14)

Through this story and many others like it, God is saying, "Be quiet and trust Me." We need to practice being quiet and trusting God.

Something in your life is going on right now and it hurts. It is painful. It might even be scary. What should you do? Be quiet and trust the Lord. You say, "Yes, but you should see my house..." Be still and trust the Lord. "I'm not making it financially, the recession is killing me." Be still and trust the Lord. That is the best thing that we can do. That is what God is teaching all of these people. God is saying, "If you can be quiet and trust Me, then I can step in and bring deliverance in the midst of the darkness."

When you think God is near, He is nearer.

As close as you think God is in the dark time, He is closer. When the Israelits saw the mountains rising up on either sides the ocean tide before them and the dust storm of the Egyptians pursuing them, God saw it too. He knew exactly what He was going to do, though the Hebrews didn't know what God was going to do. Remember, God is the Divine Lapidary. He knows where to make the cut to split the rough stone. He also knew where to make the cut to divide the Red sea. God just took His finger and made a path through the Red Sea. There you go, just walk on through. What's the problem? This is no challenge for God. God can run His finger through an ocean and split it in two. The people were not thinking with God, they were thinking in fear. We need to ask ourselves, "How big is my God?"

The size of your God determines the size of your goals.

If you have a small God, you're going to have a small life. If you have a big God, then you are going to have a large life.

The Israelites were in the darkest time. That is the time to remember this Old Testament song.

"Though I walk in the midst of trouble, You will revive me;" (Psalm 138:7) Perhaps you have a dog who loves holidays, except for July fourth, when the sounds of fireworks fill the air. He trembles and shakes in fear. That little dog can't change the fireworks but he can find comfort and security in your arms. He knows where to run. He knows where to hide and be comforted, in his master's arms.

Dear reader, perhaps you are in the midst of fireworks and you are struggling. It's painful. There are some things going on in your life that are beyond your control. The tumult is deafening. Let God console you. Be still, be silent, and watch the deliverance of the Lord.

"You will stretch forth Your hand against the wrath of my enemies, And Your right hand will save me." (Psalm 138:7)

The deeper the darkness the greater the deliverance!

A revisit to Job

Satan came to God and said; *"Does Job fear God for nothing?"* (Job 1:9) In other words, God, doesn't Job love You, respect You, and worship You because You have given him so much? There is a reason, God, why he reverences You. You have made him the wealthiest man in all the earth. Job is going to teach us the deeper the darkness, the greater the deliverance.

"Have You not made a hedge about him and his house and all that he has, on every side? You have blessed the work of his hands, and his possessions have increased in the land." Job 1:9-10

God said to Satan, do what you will but spare his life. Job became this test, this experiment, this demonstration of authentic worship. God was going to show Satan, the angels, and all of us what real worship looks like.

"Now on the day when his sons and his daughters were eating and drinking wine in their oldest brother's house, a messenger came to Job and said, "The oxen were plowing and the donkeys feeding beside them, and the Sabeans attacked and took them. They also slew the servants with the edge of the sword, and I alone have escaped to tell you."

"While he was still speaking, another also came and said, "The fire of God fell from heaven and burned up the sheep and the servants and consumed them, and I alone have escaped to tell you."

"While he was still speaking, another also came and said, "The Chaldeans formed three bands and made a raid on the camels and took them and slew the servants with the edge of the sword, and I alone have escaped to tell you."

"While he was still speaking, another also came and said, "Your sons and your daughters were eating and drinking wine in their oldest brother's house, and behold, a great wind came from across the wilderness and struck the four corners of the

house, and it fell on the young people and they died, and I alone have escaped to tell you." Job 1:13-19

What an awful course of events. It seemed like every passing moment brought a tragedy to the family of Job. Can there be any thicker darkness? Let's watch Job's response.

"Then Job arose and tore his robe and shaved his head, and he fell to the ground and worshiped."

Job 1:20

The tearing of the robe and shaving of the head was an ancient, mid-Eastern expression of extreme grief. "I am nothing. I have been reduced to ashes." Perhaps Job even felt that he had nothing to live for, because everything he lived for had been taken away.

People do get to that place. They actually get to a place where they think, "Everything I lived for, I don't have anymore. So why live?" They begin this journey of self destruction. For them, life has lost its meaning and value. What is really sad is that kind of thinking is finding its way into the minds of our young people. Through a course of unfortunate events, such as parental divorce, abandonment, rejection, bullying, or losing the battle with drugs, they don't feel like life is worth living. They have no sense of value. That is why it is so important for parents to instill value into their children. Young people seek and need affirmation from their parents more than anything else.

So Job arose, tore his robe, and shaved his head. He then did a surprising thing. He did something that not many people or anyone else would do. He fell to the ground and he worshipped.

How could he do this? How could Job enter into the deepest of the darkness and fall to the ground and worship God? This is how, and this is not going to be easy to receive, Job saw the hand behind the shining swords of the Sabeans. Whose hand? The hand of God. He saw that same hand behind the lightning flash that consumed the crops. He knew it was in the great wind that leveled the home of his children. Job knew the darkness of night was not an end in itself, but it merely set up a backdrop for the beauty of the stars to shine. Job is such an amazing man that he could recognize the hand of God in the course of these events.

Job is telling us that if God is letting this happen, it is good enough for me. I know that this does not sound normal. It may even border on lunacy. But notice Job's remarks at the end of it all.

"Naked I came from my mother's womb," (Job 1:21) When I came into the world; I had nothing and was completely dependent.

"And naked I shall return there." (Job 1:21) When I go out of this world, I will go out with nothing. Whatever I have in between, is the grace of God. God has given me something, for a time. God has given me someone, for a time. Dear reader, I know this is hard to understand. Someone has a child, just for a time. Someone else has a deep friendship, just for a time. Another has their health, just for a time. Job is saying whatever I had in the middle, is all what God has given me.

"The LORD gave and the LORD has taken away. Blessed be the name of the LORD." Job 1:21

Blessed be God. God gave me something that I didn't deserve and I had it for a number of years. In His perfect timing, He just took it all away. Blessed be the name of the Lord.

"Though I walk in the <u>midst</u> of trouble, You will revive me;" (Psalm 138:7) To be revived is to come alive! I can be surrounded by mountains, chased by soldiers with an impassable sea in front of me, and God can make me alive! I can be out of

work and God can make me alive. I can be on my sick bed and God can make me alive! I can be in the middle of a difficult divorce and God can make me alive. God is bigger. If He can put His finger through the Red Sea, split it and dry the ground, don't you think He can breathe His life into you?

"Through all this Job did not sin <u>nor did he blame God</u>." (Job 1:22) Job did not condemn God for the things that had happened in his life. Why not? Because God is good, all the time. Because God is love, all the time. Because every time you look at the cross you realize, Wow, look at what God did for me! He let His Son suffer and die on the cross, for me! God entered into His own darkness when His dear beloved Son was being brutally killed on that Roman cross. In the deepest darkness of His own life, Jesus could say, "Forgive them." Through this, He gave me Eternal Life. And whatever He has done, it is more than I deserve.

With all of that knowledge, do you think you could let God have His way in your life? Hopefully, it wouldn't be to the degree of Job. It wouldn't have to be. Could you give Him your heart the way Job did?

The deliverance from his darkness.

In the third chapter, we saw what Job had been reduced to. He lost his home, his children, his servants and livestock, even his health.

"The LORD restored the fortunes of Job when he prayed for his friends" (Job 42:10) Job had some friends that came along side him but instead of comforting him, they condemned him. They told him that he had brought this calamity upon himself. So, Job prayed for them, not himself. The threshold of discouragement is when you start

49

making it about yourself. Job wasn't an "Oh me oh my" kind of guy. It was at this point that the deliverance began!

"And the LORD increased all that Job had twofold." (Job 423:10) God gave Job twice as much as he had previously.

"Then all his brothers and all his sisters and all who had known him before came to him, and they ate bread with him in his house; and they consoled him and comforted him for all the adversities that <u>the LORD had brought on him</u>. And each one gave him one piece of money, and each a ring of gold.

The LORD blessed the latter days of Job more than his beginning; and he had 14,000 sheep and 6,000 camels and 1,000 yoke of oxen and 1,000 female donkeys.

He had seven sons and three daughters.

In all the land no women were found so fair as Job's daughters; and their father gave them inheritance among their brothers.

After this, Job lived 140 years, and saw his sons and his grandsons, four generations.

And Job died an old man and full of days."

(Job 42:10-17)

Job had a complete life. Look at Job in your times of darkness. Remember, that when you think God is near, He is nearer than you think, and He is already working. God knows what He is going to do. Sit back, be still, trust him, and let Him show you beauty in your darkness.

May God Bless You.

David P. Therrien

§

Invitation   **THE GOSPEL MESSAGE**

The word "gospel" means good news. The good news is that God has reconciled the world back to Himself through the sacrifice of His dear Son, Jesus Christ.

Invitations to salvation:

John 3:3 Truly, truly, I say to you, unless one is born again he cannot see the kingdom of God."

John 3:6 That which is born of the flesh is flesh, and that which is born of the Spirit is spirit.

John 3:15 Whoever believes, will in Him have eternal life.

John 3:16 "For God so loved the world, that He gave His only begotten Son, that whoever believes in Him shall not perish, but have eternal life.

John 3:17 For God did not send the Son into the world to judge the world, but that the world might be saved through Him.

Romans 10:9 If you confess with your mouth Jesus *as* Lord, and believe in your heart that God raised Him from the dead, you will be saved;

Romans 10:10 With the heart a person believes, resulting in righteousness, and with the mouth he confesses, resulting in salvation.

Romans 10:11 For the Scripture says, "WHOEVER BELIEVES IN HIM WILL NOT BE DISAPPOINTED."

I John 4:15 Whoever confesses that Jesus is the Son of God, God abides in him, and he in God.

I John 5:1 Whoever believes that Jesus is the Christ is born of God, and whoever loves the Father loves the *child* born of Him.

These Scriptures reveal to us that God's desire for mankind is to acknowledge their sin and need for a Savior. He then offers us forgiveness and eternal life. If you read these Scriptures above in honesty and humility, you will sense God inviting and calling you into a relationship with Him.

If you have already responded and are presently in that relationship with Him, keep walking with Him. If you are not yet in that relationship, please read these Scriptures with an open heart and then ask God to reveal Himself to you. He will be glad to do so.

Bonus Truth

Great truths are clearly bought, the common truths,
    Such as men give and take from day to day,
Come in the common walk of easy life,
    Blown by the careless wind across our way.

Great truths are greatly won, not found by chance,
    Nor wafted on the breath of summer dream,
But grasped in the great struggle of the soul,
    Hard buffeting with adverse wind and stream.

But in the day of conflict, fear and grief,
    When the strong hand of God, put forth in might,
Plows up the subsoil of the stagnant heart,
    And brings the imprisoned truth seed to the light.

Wrung from the troubled spirit, in hard hours,
    Of weakness, solitude, perchance of pain.
Truth springs like harvest from the well-plowed field,
    And the soul feels it has not wept in vain.

Anonymous

§

Strange and difficult indeed
We may find it,
But the blessing that we need
Is behind it.

Quotable Quotes

The man who has seen much affliction will not readily part with the Word of God.

William Taylor

For even as one for taking shelter from the rain beneath a tree may find on its branches fruit which he looked not for.

William Taylor

God is going to test me with delays.

C.G. Trumbull

Providence has a thousand keys to open a thousand sundry doors for the deliverance of his own.

George MacDonald

No anxiety ought to be found in a believer.

George Mueller

Nothing tests the Christian character more than to have some evil thing said about him.

A.B. Simpson

In order to grow in grace, we must be much alone.

Andrew Bonar

It has been said that no great work in literature or science was ever wrought by a man who did not love solitude.

Anonymous

God never gives feeling to enable us to trust Him. But He gives feeling when He sees that we trust Him.

Anonymous

The most deeply taught Christians are generally those who have been brought into the searching fires of deep-soul anguish.

Anonymous

§

Questions for Discussion

Ch.1 "Why the Darkness?
1. How would you describe some of the dark situations you have been in?

2. Were you able to find God there?

3. If so, what revelation did He give you?

Ch.2 "Why Pain?"
1. What blessings have you experienced from the darkness?

2. How do you feel when you think about being a precious jewel in God's eyes but He has some work to do on you to bring out your brightness?

3. As a rough cut diamond, what flaws do you see God working on to chip away?

Ch. 3 "Seeing God in the Darkness"
1. Give an example of how you can be like the nightingale singing in the darkness.

2. What was so special about Paul and Silas in comparison with the other prisoners in the Roman dungeon?

3. Why do you think we have to get rid of grudges and change our perspective in order to see God?

Ch. 4 "Deliverance in the Darkness"
1. What does it mean to be "in the midst of trouble"?

2. Do you think you could build your faith the next time you are in the darkness? How?

3. If you knew someone who saw no value in life, what would you tell them?

Other Resources

See Dave's website at www.inspiringbooks.org for more inspiring materials.

§

Acknowledgements

A special thank you to Kathryn Regan fand my lovely wife, Donna for proofreading this book to get it ready for press.
Also, a thank you to Eugene Carvalho (New Wine Ministries) for introducing me to the reality of publishing and for helping me to bring my first book to completion.

§

NOTES

NOTES

NOTES